PURITY

WRITTEN BY:
ADDIE WHITTAKER & LACEY WHITTAKER

Edited by Lil Barcaski and Linda Hinkle

Published by: GWN Publishing

www.GWNPublishing.com

Cover Design: Kristina Conatser Captured by KC Design

ISBN: 979-8-9863922-3-3

DEDICATION

This is to all those mothers and daughters out there who encourage each other to seek Jesus with their whole heart.

We would love to acknowledge Liv Whittaker a daughter and a sister. She always pushes us to be better and gives us truth with a sweet smile.

ABOUT THE BOOK

Purity is something we should all long for in this world. It's hard to feel pure. With knowing truth and what Jesus says it's possible, we share what we feel pure means to us along with character, freedom, trusting God, miracles and healing, relationships and peace.

Do you ever find yourself in discontent, disappointed or a loss of joy? I know I do sometimes. A lingering feeling or funk will come over me. I try not to stay in it long. I find myself wanting the promises that God spoke to happen now. So, when my patience of waiting on His perfect timing runs out, I become very discontent. The beginning and the end are very exciting. The middle is what I struggle with. It's the middle when our faith is tested. I hear Him say, do you trust me? Yes Lord, I trust and believe what You have spoken over me. Enjoy each day. Enjoy the journey. It's a lifetime of growth. A heart yielded in love and obedience to our precious Father.

PURE

FREE — not controllable, capable of choosing
for yourself

> *"Run as fast as you can from all the*
> *ambitions and lusts of youth; and*
> *chase after all that is pure. Whatever*
> *builds up your faith and deepens your*
> *love must become your holy pursuit.*
> *And live in peace with all those who*
> *worship our Lord Jesus with pure*
> *hearts."*
>
> 2 Timothy 2:22 *TPT*

It's hard to be pure in this world, but you can do anything with the Lord. In my own words, being pure in this world means to keep following Jesus even when it's hard. Because, when it's hard, there is always going to be a lesson or a good outcome during the situation or after. So, when it's hard, I just start praying and thanking Him for what He has given me.

"For this is how much God loved the world—He gave His one and only, unique Son as a gift. So, now everyone who believes in Him will never perish but experience everlasting life."

John 3:16 TPT

"Wherever your treasure is, there the desires of your heart will also be."

Matthew 6:21 NLT

Lord, please give me my full hearts desires. First, remove any desire not of Your will or Your way. Set my heart to treasure You foremost. Let my treasure only be found in You and then my desires shall start flowing from the true source of life.

Prayer can mean so many things. One day it's crying out for help, another minute it could be worshiping in awe and in full health. One hour, prayer is intercession for a friend, or, heaven help me, forgive the worst of them. Prayer, what is it to you? To me it's something I would never want to lose. Prayer is a special gift, a communication from us to Him. A communion, there is none other like this.

REST AND RESTORE

Do you ever go through life chasing dreams, kids, lifestyles, things, status, only to find yourself worn down, depressed, defeated, unloved, insecure? I do. I feel like it takes a minute, an hour, a day, or a week when I choose to focus on all these things and not on Jesus. He says lay down those burdens and cares, and comes to me, saying follow me and I will give you rest. ***Thank you, Prince of Peace for this unexplainable rest and restoration only You can give. Amen.***

REST - stop, lie down, ease.

RESTORATION - mend, renew, heal.

This world could be so different if this world could see truth. Do you ever wonder what happened and why they chose not too? This world could all be saved if we turned from our evil ways, looked up, and called on His everlasting name. **This, oh this, I pray.**

UNSPEAKABLE JOY

REJOICE - gladden, great delight

*I have told you these things so that
my joy and delight may be in you,
and that your joy may be made full
and complete and overflowing.*

John 15:11 *AMP*

There is no other joy like this. Joy in the Lord is so much different than joy in the world. The Lord gives us this special feeling and it feels like you just accomplished something really big at work, school, or whatever it may be. You will notice that this joy is the best feeling. It's almost like you don't know what just happened. So, always remember to thank the Lord if you get joy in the little things, or the big things, because it all happens for a reason.

Though you have not seen Him, you love Him; and though you do not even see Him now, you believe and trust in Him and you greatly rejoice and delight with inexpressible and glorious joy,

1 Peter 1:8 *AMP*

KEEP IT SIMPLE. Keep it sacred. Keep it holy in all the tight spaces. When there comes a time to choose evil or good, look and know that He would and could do it all over again to save our soul, to save us from our sin. Look to His eyes of love and grace and choose to live like Him today.

BREAK FREE. Break loose everything that's in you that does not produce fruit. Produce truth to speak from your lips. Live a life full of repentance. This will boost and break bondage, you see. This repentance is a key to everlasting victory and peace.

Do you ever feel misunderstood, persecuted, hated, or lonely doing the will of God? Hearing the will of God? Speaking the will of God? Sharing the will of God? Does your family, friends, or hometown mock, throw shade, or simply just don't believe in your way? It's okay! You're in good company. Jesus walked in this too. They persecuted Him, won't they you? Shake your sandals, forgive and repent. Serve our Father for He loves to see us overcome and walk along so very strong. Give grace, give love, and friend, move on.

> *"Then He went out from there and came to His own country, and His disciples followed Him. And when the Sabbath had come, He began to teach in the synagogue. And many hearing Him were astonished, saying, "Where did this Man get these things? And what wisdom is this which is given to Him, that such mighty works are performed by His hands! Is this not the carpenter, the Son of Mary, and brother of James, Joseph, Judah, and Simon? And are not His sisters here with us?"*

So, they were offended at Him. But Jesus said to them, "A prophet is not without honor except in his own country, among his own relatives, and in his own house." Now He could do no mighty work there, except that He laid His hands on a few sick people and healed them. And He marveled because of their unbelief. Then He went about the villages in a circuit, teaching."

Mark 6:1-6 *NKJV*

What do you find yourself caring about? Is it the wrong things, the right things, or maybe good things, but you care too much in the wrong way? Does it make you hurt or make you sick? Do you worry too much and never repent? May we ask ourselves, is this for the kingdom or to promote ourselves or our children? Are we too focused on them and how they win? Or are we raising them up to look past wealth and recognition? It's hard to face our ugly, prideful ways, but when we do, He gives great grace to see us change.

CHARACTER. *We go through to build our character. To honor You we go through. To build our character, to honor and glorify truth. Character is for You. Character, come and ring true.*

PROTECTOR

GUARDIAN - one who cares

The Lord is always by your side even if you don't see it or feel it. He sees every need you or your family may have. He is a protector.

You will be the inner strength of all Your people, Yahweh, the mighty protector of all, and the saving strength for all Your anointed ones.

Psalms 28:8 *TPT*

When we fight, when we wrestle, when we go to bat another round. When we can't seem to lay down all those selfish crowns not of You. When we keep on keeping on to pursue things that don't matter to You. Strike us, help us, shake us to see, those are death and You are life to thee. Those worldly crowns we chase, those tired lives we face. When we run ragged to feel defeat, stop, look up, and receive the only thing that gives true peace. The only one that loves and shows grace, our Father smiling to say, you made it, you won. Now, go along in a whole new way, this my child is a brand-new way.

Stillness, quiet, calm, peace. The stillness in the air the stillness in our cares. Jesus, You take them all away when we choose to seek Your face. Cast them down leave them there, it's Your voice we long to hear.

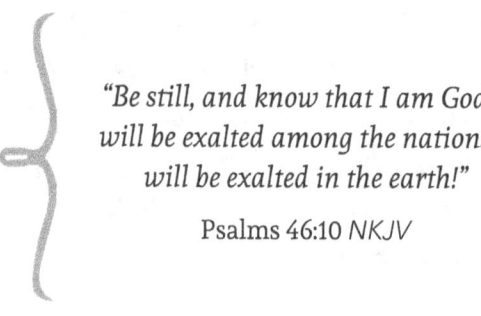

"Be still, and know that I am God; I
will be exalted among the nations, I
will be exalted in the earth!"

Psalms 46:10 NKJV

You will know them by the fruit they produce. Is it good? Is it bad? Is it steady? Is it glad? Is it lost? Is it found? The evidence is the fruit bore. You will see the evidence in how they speak, how they love, how they share, and how they live. Watch for it, believe for it, it's the evidence shown. I find myself thinking things in my head and allowing it to filter into my heart. *Take it out Lord, before I come apart. Show me truth, save me from the deceit, save me. Help my eyes and heart to see.*

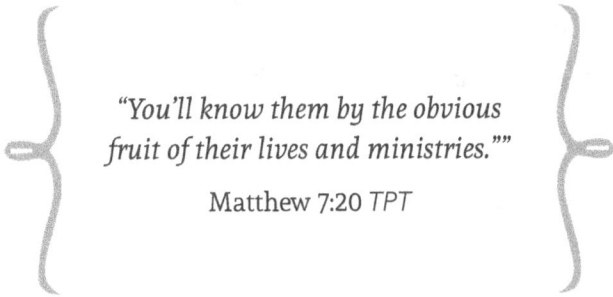

"You'll know them by the obvious
fruit of their lives and ministries.""

Matthew 7:20 *TPT*

> "You can spot them by their actions,
> for the fruits of their character will
> be obvious. You won't find sweet
> grapes hanging on a thorn bush, and
> you'll never pick good fruit from a
> tumbleweed."
>
> Matthew 7:16 *TPT*

You always see the good in us. How is this so? You always see the good and know we should let go. You always see the good and teach us to obey. Help us see this life is ours to take, ours to win, ours to never give up, the prize worth living to one day be with You in that place called eternity. That's my faith.

DEFENDER

GUARD - protector

God is my defender, there is no doubt about it. I thank Him every day for what He has given me. God is going to be there when you need Him most.

He loves you.

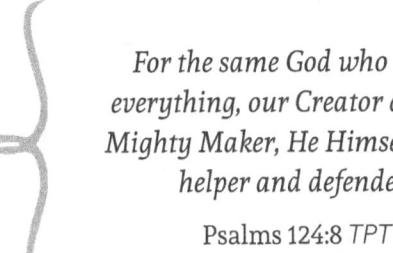

For the same God who made everything, our Creator and our Mighty Maker, He Himself is our helper and defender!

Psalms 124:8 *TPT*

Let go. Forgive. Release the offense. Have closure, heal, and move forward.

Do you wonder what our children will grow up and see? Do you wonder what lives they will live to serve thee? Do you wonder if they will suffer and fail in their insecurities? Do you wonder if they love Jesus more than they love you and me? Wonder no more, we have a king. A king that loves them more than anything. So, today, give them to Him, watch and see. Feel the release of a mother and father set free. Giving them to Him, our only protector and peace, we are giving them up to be fathers and mothers honoring Thee.

SECURE

SAFE - free from harm

From my walk with the Lord. He has been a good, good, good, God. He has kept me safe from this world and from everybody around me that tries to hurt me. So, I continue to walk with Him.

Yahweh has established His throne in heaven; His kingdom rules the entire universe.

Psalms 103:19 *TPT*

Truth wins. Love wins. Grace wins. Hope wins. Fights are fought and easy to do, but at the end of it, you always lose. So, choose His way, the only way to win. Hope, love, peace, and a big grin.

Be obedient. Trust His love. Go the extra to fall and be hurt. Be humble. Go the extra to lose but gain because at the end of the day it's His grace that reigns.

Acknowledge hurt but don't stay there. Be love, but don't be overrun by fear. See doubt, but have hope that overcomes. Be grace, be one. *You are worthy. You are true. You are beautiful and loved. You are you. Yes, He chose you!* Live like it today. Cast the rest away. Live like you are known because you have a God who loves to show. You are His child. Live and know, you are His child that He chose.

OBEY

FOLLOW - succeed, supervene

Always obey the Lord, even when it's hard to, or maybe you just simply don't want to at the time. It's going to be so much better if you do and always remember to trust Him because He will lead you through anything. *You are safe in His arms.*

> "In that I command you today to love the Lord, your God, to walk [that is, to live each and every day] in His ways and to keep His commandments and His statutes and His judgments (precepts), so that you will live and multiply, and that the Lord, your God will bless you in the land which you are entering to possess."

Deuteronomy 30:16 *AMP*

We are sinners, we are lost, we are paid and bought. Call on Him to live, call on Him and see. Call on Jesus, the only one, call on Him and walk along.

> *"But whatever [word] comes out of the mouth comes from the heart, and this is what defiles and dishonors the man."*
>
> Matthew 15:18 *AMP*

This verse made me think. What kind of things are coming out of my mouth? Is it words of life or death? Encouragement or persecution? Goodness or gossip? Fake or truth? Hatred or love? Judging or grace? Hurt or forgiveness? Whatever is in your heart will come out from your mouth. *I pray a deep cleanse of my heart and a daily repentance of all these evil things that enter in. For our flesh is weak but spirit is strong and able to overcome the enemy's schemes.*

Do you ever just say, why God, why? Do you ever wonder where He is? Do you ever wonder why you walk through hard things? I do. This was a tough, tough month. I heard Him say this morning to let go, surrender, quit worshipping your problems and insecurities. Step out of that pit you are in and worship Me, your loving Father. The one that cares, hears, loves and doesn't cause fear.

So, this morning I stepped over, casted down my fears, and now I can look up and not around. Praying a blessing over you all today and if you are in a pit, I pray you look up and see our loving Father's face.

Do you have faith? Do you trust? Do you look up and say, was that You? Do you walk a mile and always choose? Do you ever question, but what if? Do you ask questions on how this even adds up? How a Father could send His son to die a painful death for those of us who may never believe in Him. How does this make sense to a sinner like me to be totally set free? These questions I may have asked, but I've read the truth, and was free at last. *I have the faith, hope, and trust. Thank you, Holy Spirit, for showing me wisdom and love.*

Be confident and speak. Be obedient and pray on your knees. Do what He has called you to do with a mind that chooses not to lose.

FEAR • WORRY • RELEASE

I woke up at 1:50am, wide awake. Usually, this means God is trying to get my attention because I love my sleep. This rarely happens. So, I asked Lord, what are You trying to get through to me? He says, release your worry and fear. There's a little left in there that needs to go. **Release, go, and repent.** I would love to say this is really easy, but with my past panic attacks and anxiety, sometimes this little bit roars up inside of me. Now, the fear and worry are far and in between, but I could do better at casting it down and releasing instead of holding on and lingering in it for longer than I should. When we repent, we can release sin whether it's known or the unknown He reveals to us. He will show us sin we may not even realize as sin. I pray for anyone struggling today with this, you would be able to surrender and repent and have the amazing peace Jesus wants to give us.

Lord, I let go of this sickness. I am free, I am unblocked, I will flow with health and the Holy Spirit. I am healed in my body. No more sickness, no more pain. I am sorry body. I am sorry for abusing you, for talking bad to you, not appreciating you. I am sorry. Forgive me, oh Lord. I repent and will watch my thoughts and words. I will praise and not curse. Thank you, God. I will be gentle and kind to myself. I will be in happiness, peace, and joy.

ANCHORED

FIRM - secure, not weak, non-movable

Anchored. Being anchored with Jesus means no matter what, if you have the hope, the peace, the trust, the joy, you will not be moved. If you are anchored, there are going to be many people against you, but also there are going to be very few people who are going to be for you.

> *We have this certain hope, like a strong, unbreakable anchor holding our souls to God Himself. Our anchor of hope is fastened to the mercy seat in the heavenly realm beyond the sacred threshold.*
>
> Hebrews 6:19 *TPT*

If you stay with Jesus, He will be your mighty anchor, with Him no one can move you. In the end, it doesn't matter who's with you and who's not. The only thing that matters is your relationship with Jesus.

> *The wicked are blown away by every stormy wind. But when a catastrophe comes, the lovers of God have a secure anchor.*
>
> Proverbs 10:25 *TPT*

These days it's hard to do. It's hard to listen and show truth. It's hard not to fall into the trap. It's hard not to live and never look back. It's hard, yes, this life is hard. ***He never promised it would be easy, but He did say we could run to Him to find peace and strength. He is a God of everything.***

Are you dealing with health concerns, worry, defeat? One of my close friends, who I love dearly, has been struggling this past week with some. As I look at her, it breaks my heart seeing what she is going through. He placed a song on my heart at just the right time, placed her in my thoughts, and gave me a word that she will be alright. When? I don't know. How long? Don't we always wonder? I do. When I know, like I know, He can heal her in one moment, this could be all done and her health be restored like brand new. When? It's His timing. He gave me a sweet word I can hold on to until I see it with my eyes. I will believe it, because I know He is our healer.

I pray over anyone that is sick in the body today to be healed in the name of Jesus. Keep your eyes fixed on Him. He will hear you. Go to Him and simply ask. I hear Him say, you shall be healed. The Lord is good and almighty.

Peace, my favorite fruit of the spirit. Peace, where do you go when my mind wanders out of control? Peace, how I love you. Peace, oh peace, come back soon. Do you ever struggle with not having peace? I do. This is one thing I desire always. I have lived through anxiety, worry, and panic attacks. My peace is everything to me. When my mind wreaks havoc, and goes into an endless pit, I hear my Father say... Do you know real rest? Like the rest beyond rest? *Go into the deep of rest. Have peace, sit with me, and let me lead. I will lead you into deep peace.* I vision a pasture where I can lie down in peace and graze there and forever be. Let go of control and find rest in our heavenly Father.

Do you hate the unlovable and throw shade at the hurting ones? Do you misunderstand what was aimed for your growth? Did it take a slice of your pride? Did you rare up and want to fight? That flesh loves to win, but the spirit says, let go, forgive, and love them.

Start small and stay simple. Make a habit and watch it grow. Start small and stay simple. You will see it's the small things that one day turns into a great thing.

What do you think of torment, agony, despair? Do you look around and wonder if He even cares? I believe those hits come and run deep. They come to steal our peace. What we do, how we perceive. How will we choose to be: stay in our pride and defeat, or let go, be humble, and see. Pain, suffering, and despair. **We have the strength to overcome all cares. Look up to Him with eyes to see. Not what's left but trust in Thee.**

> "Because of the surpassing greatness and extraordinary nature of the revelations [which I received from God], for this reason, to keep me from thinking of myself as important, a thorn in the flesh was given to me, a messenger of Satan, to torment and harass me—to keep me from exalting myself!"

2 Corinthians 12:7 *AMP*

Do the hard things, and do them well. Say you're sorry, and go on to tell. Live at peace with others, and love them, love them. Love them as our Father shows us how to love. Care for them. Treat them with respect. At the end of the day what's really left? A pat on the back, a warm hug, a friend calling to just check-up. Community. We need a loving community honoring our Father in Heaven that sees. He made us to live together and serve Him and be well, chosen Heaven sent. He made us to be strong and love at all cost, give up ourselves as He died on that cross. **Love. Forgive and be forgiven.** That's His will for us to live and be given.

LETTING GO. Do you ever hold on a little too long? Do you ever hang on, crying all along, knowing you should move, but choose to stay at the view you are in? Are you safe, secure, comfortable with, to miss what's in store and heaven sent? **Let go today. Let go and see with eyes of faith. Let go and release the past. Let go and be free at last.**

THE PAST. Previous former things. The past. I hang on sometimes too long. Is there a new way? The past is there to remember, I see. Remember all those things You have done to set me free. The past. You can be a reckoning, or I can see the past as how far You really kept me. Pulling me through, closer to You, growth love, resurrection, made new. Past, I am no longer angry with you.

When you feel like you can't trust anymore, when you feel like you aren't good enough, when you feel like everyone is against you, look to the one above, the one who will always be by your side no matter what, the one who will never disappoint, the one who created you, the one that made you good enough, the one that is for you when everyone is against you, the one who will never leave.

MARRIAGE. UNION. ALLIANCE. Such a holy and sacred relationship where two become one to share in such a love. It's a precious gift that is often missed when eyes aren't fixed solely on Him who made us to be in union as not one, or two, but three. This special place a marriage holds, when both choose to honor and love Him most.

"So then, they are no longer two but one flesh. Therefore, what God has joined together, let not man separate."

Matthew 19:6 *NKJV*

What do you do with all that angers and torments you? Do you hold it in until it spills out of you like a dark cold truth? Do you hide it deep down, bury it where no one sees? Keep it there until it bleeds? This can make you sick, ill feelings of destruction, defeat, bring you to your knees. If you fall there, repent, let go. *Release. Let those burdens lay at His feet.* Hold them no longer. Oh, no longer are you bound by all this death that tears you down. *Fall. Release. Smile and breathe. Look up and say thank You for saving me.*

Are you holding on? Gripping tight? Not wanting to let go? Maybe it's someone or something and you hear your loving Father say, release, release, release now, and you wonder, but how? Really, how can I release something so big? So close. I have to say we have a Father that knows what's best you see. *He knows when it's time to release. So, let go today and find peace. When you do, you will be set free.*

Are you beaten, battered, bruised, all from what the Lord has called you to do? Are you lost, lonely, scared, wondering why in the world, and does He truly care? Does He care how hard this is on you? Does He care it rips your heart in two? Why, oh why? These hard things I would say, He knows best. **Listen and obey.** You will find peace after obedience you see. You will find peace and be totally set free. He knows best, that you will see. He knows best. Trust and honor Thee. **He will love you through everything.**

Are you pure and holy when you kick and scream? Are you pure and holy when you feel defeat? Are you pure and holy when you are threatening to leave?

Are you pure and holy? What does this really mean?

Are you pure and holy as He sees? Are you pure in heart and holy from the start? Are you pure and holy? What does this mean? What is your character? What does it say? **Do you lead or pull others astray? Do you show Christ in the most loving and kind ways?**

Do you go the extra mile for a friend and say, you matter? I'm here. Night or day. Do you cheer for others? Are you selfish with pride? Do you humble yourself and give life?

Your character you build all your days. What kind of character would others have to say?

Character and truth go hand in hand. Truth withstands time you have had. Truth is what others will hold on to. Truth will withstand when all else fails. It's time. It's time to ring the bell.

LOVING

AFFECTIONATE - warm regard, loving

> *"Beloved children, our love can't be an abstract theory we only talk about, but a way of life demonstrated through our loving deeds."*
>
> 1 John 3:18 *TPT*

You hear about people saying, I love you so much, but have you really felt God's love? Well let me tell you a little about my God's love. The Lord's love is really unexplainable, but I am going to try my best. It's like something you have never felt, it never stops.

He loves us so much, that He died on the cross for all of us.

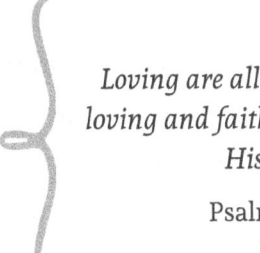

*Loving are all the ways of Yahweh,
loving and faithful for those who keep
His covenant.*

Psalms 25:10 *TPT*

What is a wife without her husband? A mother without her child? Seems dark and lonely. Trying to survive. Living without Jesus. Oh, honoring Him living. I would die just to see Him.

What's to lose, this world or your faith? What do you choose in these sad days? Do you listen to the news or sit quiet and still? Know that our Father is in control and still will save us from this world and all that it throws. The hate. The punishment and all the sin. What will you choose? How will you live? I know I've made my mind up. *I will choose to believe in Him.*

Obedience. You seem harsh. You seem like my flesh wants to run but my heart knows it's a start. A step into the will of Him, not the world, not our flesh.

Obedience is a key that unlocks our dreams.

It even unlocks our insecurities because we obey. He sends down grace. We see and live in a whole new way.

MIRACLES

WONDERS - marvel, blessings, astonishment

Some miracles can happen in an instant, and some won't just happen overnight. You have to have the faith. You can't just pray for something and think it will be there the next day. It takes time to have strong, mighty faith.

God's timing is the perfect timing.

A miracle may be something you really want or something you really want to see happen.

> *From my childhood You've been my teacher, and I'm still telling everyone of Your miracle-wonders!*
>
> Psalms 71:17 *TPT*

Truth. Do you speak it? Do you show it? Do you rise up against and throw it? Do you misplace it or call it to rest? Do you sugar coat because you don't want stress?

Truth slaps you. Wakes you up. But to tell the truth, you have to grow up. Be mature. Walk in faith.

Truth tellers see with eyes of faith, with grace, with love. The truth always wins, so next time you feel fake, slap yourself and awake.

STRENGTH. Where does it come from? Do you get it from never stopping or slowing down? Do you get it for that world's crown? Do you get it from those people that cut and tear you down? I would say strength comes from many things, but at the end of the day, I ask from the one that only gives and never takes.

Where does grace come from? Do you shoot down and scowl, then turn around and ask your Father for grace but can't forgive your neighbor for treating you that way? *Grace wins every time, so forgive the ones and quit wasting your time.*

HOLY

DIVINE - divine love, divine inspiration

DEVOTED - loyalty

Jesus has a divine love for all of us, no matter what we have done, that will never change. We have to have a divine inspiration to be like Him. He is the most powerful, most loving, most caring, most trustworthy God. He will do anything to help you and your family. He is holy, righteous, and all around a great God. All that we have to do is pray and be in thanksgiving all of our days.

To live my life by your righteous rules has been my holy and lifelong commitment.

Psalms 119:106 *TPT*

Keep running. Keep running, asking Him to lead. Keep running with eyes of victory. Keep running. Keep running this race He's called to be. Keep running. Keep running past your insecurities. He's building you up. Wait and see. Keep running. Keep running. It's all for you and me.

A wrecking ball. Out to get. Out to take from all of this. A wrecking ball. Those evil snares. A wrecking ball. It doesn't care. Save your life from all of this. The wrecking ball doesn't seem to miss.

Don't wreck your life to one day be almost at death before you call upon Him to rest.

Don't waste your life. Don't waste one breath. Live this life like there's nothing left because the days will pass and you will look back. Don't look back and say, I regret living that way.

Breathe. Breathe. Breathe. I say breathe. Breathe. Breathe in a whole new way. Breathe that breath. The next one you take, breathe in Jesus. He is here to stay.

How do you sing His goodness? How do you praise His name? When you are walking through so much pain, so much hurt, so much offense, how do you sing your way through and know He loves you even in your darkest hard times, how do you? *I choose. I choose to say, You are my love, my faith, my everything.* It's a choice, I say I choose to sing Your name all day long. I choose to believe You make me strong. I choose to lay aside the rest and know You have blessed me and will see me through, Lord, God, Jesus, Holy Spirit. *I choose. I choose. I choose You every time, every way. I choose You. I choose to praise Your name in the good and the bad. I choose to be glad.*

HONESTY. Do you find it hard to be honest sometimes? Do you find it hard to not tell a little white lie to cover, to cover you? Maybe you are trying to cover some hard truths? I know, it's very hard for me too, but there's the spirit inside that guides and provides to do the hard things. ***Tell the truth, for when you do, you shall never lose.***

TRUST

CONFIDE - protection, confidence

It is very hard to trust God in this world. There are always going to be people to tell you the wrong things. Very few people know right from wrong. **One thing for sure is that there is one God and one God only.**

The hard part is the trust part, the trust that you are going to make it through, the trust that God is real, the trust that you're loved, maybe when you don't feel it. It is very important to trust God through anything, the good or the bad.

> *Don't be pulled in different directions*
> *or worried about a thing. Be*
> *saturated in prayer throughout*
> *each day, offering your faith-filled*
> *requests before God with overflowing*
> *gratitude. Tell Him every detail of*
> *your life,*
>
> Philippians 4:6 *TPT*

KINDNESS. What does being kind mean to you? Is it smiling or lending a helping hand? Is it going the extra mile when the mile wasn't part of the plan?

Being kind, being selfless, can be an easy thing to do, but what about being kind to the ones that despise you? That's the true test. You see, being kind to the ones that don't believe, maybe they are irritated by you.

Be kind and see how it grows you.

WALK CLEAN. WALK HOLY. What does this mean? What does this look like? I would say, wake up with a surrendered, yielded heart. Wake up. That's a start. Go through your day meditating in prayer. Go through your day knowing he cares.

Yield.

Repent.

The pride. The lies. The way of life.

Repent.

Be clean.

Walk holy with the one that calls us, free to be holy, because of He.

Sin. Why do we sin? Do we choose it? Is it fun? Are we blind and do not see? Why do we choose this way, the hard way, the wrong way? Why do we offend and continue wrong doing?

I believe when our flesh fails, when we do not surrender to God's will, but walk in our own.

Maybe it's easier for some to sin and not change? Maybe it's a game? Where do you want to be? In the middle? Half in? Half out? Playing both sides? Do you even want to try? Or do you want to choose now to repent and bow, change your ways, and ask for His grace to see another day, to truly live in forgiveness and walk out of sin.

Ask Him.

Ask daily.

He will be there every step, every day. He will be there when you choose His way.

MIGHTY

POWERFUL - prestige, significant

I am a mighty child of God. When the Lord says that I am a mighty child of God, it encourages me to push harder at knowing Him, telling about Him, and showing Him throughout every day of my life.

Then my fears will dissolve into limitless joy; my whole being will overflow with gladness because of your mighty deliverance.

Psalms 35:9 *TPT*

Evil. Wickedness. Thief and destruction. Where does it come from? How did you fall in such a pit and miss this life He has for you? How did you turn and go the wrong way? Was it over time of not calling on His name? Did you never know Him this way? Were you not taught His great love and grace?

It's never too late to turn from all of it. It's never too late to give up the sin you live in.

It's never too late. Go right now. Give Him your life.

Trust and be about the King that has come to save. The King that died to take our place on that cross. He bore our sins so one day we could live with Him again.

Turn away. Repent. He's waiting for you. Turn. See the light of truth.

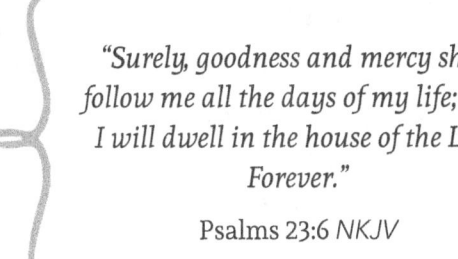

"Surely, goodness and mercy shall follow me all the days of my life; And I will dwell in the house of the Lord Forever."

Psalms 23:6 *NKJV*

He is merciful. He is faithful. He is good. Oh, so good! Don't look at the world for His goodness.

Look to Him. Choose Him.

His spirit will come upon and live inside you when you choose. He will show you truth and all the good things. You won't find them here.

Look up. Praise His name.

All the heavenly things can be given to you. Ask Him. He is faithful and true.

Do you ever feel distracted, annoyed, disturbed, absent, with noise? I want to flip over the sounds of clanging buttons in the dryer, or a paper bag in the car that my child is messing with, or maybe it's loud noises that come unexpectedly, I don't know. Random noises just get me. They get me and take me to another level of aggravation.

I think the enemy and the world loves to keep us distracted or annoyed, because if he can't get us to do things we use to do, say things we shouldn't say, or hurt us in a different way, well, he will just try and annoy us and keep us distracted, because what better way to wake up or getting ready to sit and pray and have some quiet time with the Lord at home or in the car, then a big loud bang!

I would say, if this happens to you, as it does me, let it go, laugh it off, don't stay stuck in these games or ways the enemy tries to play.

Smile and go the other way and praise our Saviors name.

Mercy triumphs over judgment. Thank God for that. Thank God for all us sinners that mercy, kindness, goodness, forgiveness, triumphs over judgment, assessment ruling sentences. Thank God for mercy over judgment.

Thank God. I thank Him today for His wonderful mercy over a repentant, but sinner's flesh I live in. Thank You for Your everlasting mercy, kindness, goodness, and love.

> "There will be no mercy for those who have not shown mercy to others. But if you have been merciful, God will be merciful when He judges you."
>
> James 2:13 NLT

Be still. Be still. Be still. Be still. Be still. Hear my voice.

Be still and hear my voice.

I want to speak to you and be with you all your days. Be still. Surrender and lay all your burdens down. Be still. Look past all your doubt. Be still. I am the one that crowns. Be still. Be still. Be still. Be totally freely, peacefully still, and then you will reap the I wills.

> "Be still and know (recognize, understand) that I am God. I will be exalted among the nations! I will be exalted in the earth."
>
> Psalms 46:10 *AMP*

> "Let the one who does wrong, still do wrong; and the one who is filthy (vile, impure), still be filthy; and the one who is righteous (just, upright), still be righteous; and the one who is holy, still be holy."
>
> Revelation 22:11 *AMP*

> *"Be still before the Lord; wait patiently for Him and entrust yourself to Him; Do not fret (whine, agonize) because of him who prospers in his way, because of the man who carries out wicked schemes."*
>
> Psalms 37:7 *AMP*

I hear Him say, rest today. Rest. Stay in My loving arms and rest today. Rest. Feel My peace with the words that I speak. Feel my peace, when I say all is really going to be ok. Hold on to Me. Hold on and never let go. Now rest my children. Rest.

You are so very blessed.

BOUNDARIES. We all need boundaries. Boundaries are so important to live by with how God has called us to truly live. He set boundaries as He created this beautiful world. He wants us to set them too.

I think boundaries change often as life goes on for each one. It's always good to reevaluate your priorities and schedules.

As the world calls us to be busy, Jesus calls us to rest.

Go to Him and ask His will. Ask Him to help you set boundaries, as I know these boundaries bring me peace, love, and joy. Be well my friends. I pray He speaks so clearly to you on boundaries. Boundaries have changed my life.

*"Do you not fear Me?' says the Lord.
'Do you not tremble [in awe] in My
presence? For I have placed the sand
as a boundary for the sea. An eternal
decree and a perpetual barrier beyond
which it cannot pass. Though the
waves [of the sea] toss and break, yet
they cannot prevail [against the sand
ordained to hold them back]; Though
the waves and the billows roar, yet
they cannot cross over [the barrier].
[Is not such a God to be feared?]"*

Jeremiah 5:22 *AMP*

PRAYER. What do you think of as prayer? I think we all may think of prayer differently. You could've been taught a certain way growing up. Maybe you were never taught or have never seen prayer.

Maybe prayer is something you feel you aren't worthy of. Maybe prayer is something that seems hard. Maybe prayer is something that seems unattainable.

Prayer is rather simple. I believe my prayer life changed when I knew I could actually have a relationship with our Father. It changed. I went from asking the Lord, can You please help me get this job or bless my kids to a deeper relationship and prayer life with my best friend Jesus?

Now, I feel like prayer is an ongoing relationship I have with Him. I talk to Him all day long, and if I'm patient and quiet, surrendered and still, I hear Him talking back to me. Prayer is everything to me. Prayer is what gets me through the hard days and good days too. Prayer is my heart yielded to the Father.

Today, I would say, if you don't know prayer, sit and ask Him. Start small and go big. Just pray. This way of prayer will change your life today.

Do you have compassion? Does kindness and mercy follow you? Do you give it? It's easy to give to the lovable, but what about the ones that don't love you? What about the ones that sting you?

Compassion runs deep.

Compassion is the cross on Calvary.

Compassion is taught, but do you really get how compassion saved you and me? The compassion Jesus had on us should run through our veins. It should not be a waste. Compassion should be what makes us rise above and love. To repent and do good to men. It should be our heart, our prayers, to have compassion every day, everywhere.

The waves crash, the ocean roars, all at the sound of Your command. The beach stays still with a small will. The sand shakes, the earth quakes, the winds blow, and the storms roll. All this beauty, all the splendor. We are just passing through, seeing how You are You. You are so mighty, so big. All of this we just can't seem to fathom.

Lord, oh Lord, you are at it.

The only commitment dedication you will see from me, will be the commitment to the Lord. I'm not playing games here in this carnal world. I'm living fully, only to please the one who created me.

Will that look different to you? Maybe, if we don't line up the same, but I will always prove to be faithful to the end to what is called to me by my Father in Heaven.

He directs my steps, not man.

Joy and hope in all we do. Joy and hope. Oh, how we love you. Joy and hope. Everything seems to be joyful when we choose to look to Thee. Look to Thee with eyes of faith. Look to Thee that loves and doesn't hate. Look to Thee. So much glory there. Lord, I look to You. Heaven knows no care.

Smile, it's truth. Smile, it's you. Smile, you win. Smile and grin. Smile, you know. Smile, you show. Smile when it's all stacked up against you.

Smile, He loves you.

Smile, you win. Smile, you grin. Smile, you hold that always open door.

Smile, Jesus cares.

Smile, you can feel Him everywhere. Smile, with hope. Smile, with peace. Your savior loves you indefinitely, throughout eternity.

SECURE • SAFE • PROTECTED • CONFIDENT • SURE • SOLID • FIRM • STRONG • STEADY • UNTROUBLED

I woke up hearing Him say, stop with your insecurity, self-worth, people's opinions or lack of. Where are you searching for such things?

He said, if you look to Me, I will make you strong, able, and steady to stand against all the enemy's schemes.

Today, I shall fear the Lord and what He says, because in this, I know I will be ok.

His word is eternal, solid, and sound.

So, I will shake the enemy and lies I believed, take my Fathers hand and be in rest and thanksgiving.

I pray for anyone struggling, trying to fit in, or feeling unworthy, lost, confused, or scared, that you look to your heavenly Father that loves and cares. He will show you truth.

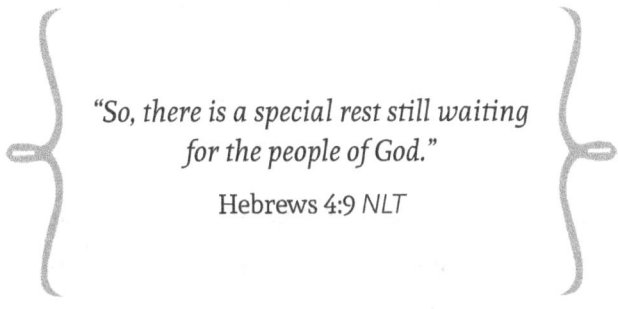

"So, there is a special rest still waiting for the people of God."

Hebrews 4:9 *NLT*

STRONG

FIRM - not weak, secure

SOLID - not interrupted, made firmly and well

What makes me feel strong, is when I am feeling down about something and I hear the voice of the Lord saying, keep going, you got this, you are almost there, persevere. Things like that make me feel strong.

> *Here's what I've learned through it all: Don't give up; don't be impatient; be entwined as one with the Lord. Be brave and courageous, and never lose hope. Yes, keep on waiting—for he will never disappoint you!*
>
> Psalms 27:14 *TPT*

Disobedience will lead you into a heavy pit of despair and state of somber. Is it always easy? No. Does it take a few pushes and nudges sometimes? Yes.

I will never have peace until I am in full obedience of the Lord's will over my life. If I choose to say yes to Jesus, every time, over the world and the flesh and never accept anything less, I have peace and direction. I have hope, even when it's hard to do so.

Lord, You have my yes. Send me.

Do you ever wake up feeling you are in a deep dark pit? This month was like a blur. Each day was another struggle and then another. The days all just ran together.

When I get tired, worn, and emotional, and when the struggle doesn't stop, I would love to say, I pray... I do pray, but I also use food as a comfort, as a vice. I've always struggled with this. Emotional eating is so real. I would eat, then feel sick, then get on the scale, feel terrible about myself, and the cycle just goes on and on and on, until you wake up and feel all this shame, and burden, and guilt you have carried. When will this all end?

I saw a friend post about this the other day and thought, wow, more people struggle with this than I ever knew. Whether you feel like you are overweight, underweight, not pretty, what do you see when you look in the mirror?

I would like to say you aren't the only one feeling this way. This cycle can break with prayer, repentance, with help from community. This cycle will break, and I pray that for anyone struggling today with body image and addiction. It's so real and it's so hard to overcome, but you can and you will, just like I know I will.

Gods timing, His perfect loving timing, a heart yielded in love and faith.

So today, love yourself where you are at, I know Jesus does.

Be well my friends, be very, very well. Healthy looks different for many people. It's not a one size fits all. Don't let the photoshopped media fool you. That's the enemy's greatest scheme.

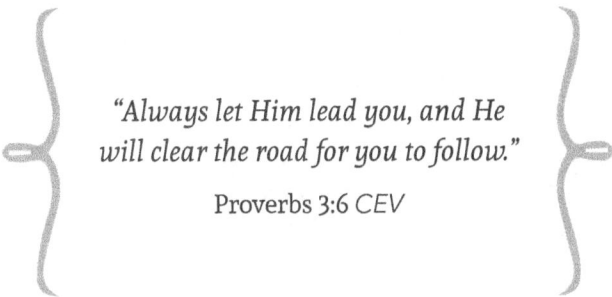

"*Always let Him lead you, and He will clear the road for you to follow.*"

Proverbs 3:6 *CEV*

UNDERSTANDING. Understanding some things can be difficult. It's not always how our human brains think, but how the Lord needs or wants us to think. We might just need to be in a resting stage and not a "let's go do everything" kind of stage.

Some things are easy to understand, but others are not. The Lord's way of thinking is always better than our human way of thinking. Understand that He has bigger plans no matter what.

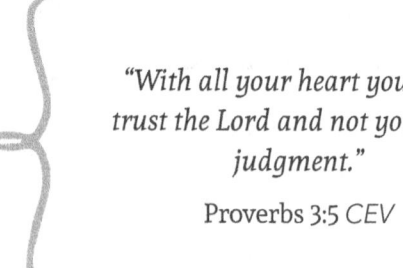

"With all your heart you must trust the Lord and not your own judgment."

Proverbs 3:5 CEV

I believe, when I let my thoughts go on and on, and don't make them stop to obey truth, and the word of the Lord, all of the sudden, I have this overwhelming fear that overcomes me like a HIT.

I would say, STOP, let them go. Go into scripture, meditate on what's good and true, and see how much He loves you.

What do you do when you are suffering so much? Do you fall in a pit and say you are done? Do you ask for help or choose to stay there? Do you wonder if anyone truly cares? Do you blame it on God, that He let this be? Do you forget how He died for you and me?

Don't be confused by what you may be dealt, our Father is loving and will always be there to help.

Call on His name. Forgive and repent. He is ready to pull you from your pit.

RESURRECTION DAY. You rose from that grave. You rose up. How could this be? A miracle our eyes could not see but by faith we believe. How could this be? You died to set us free. You died to set us free. Help us walk in that pain and agony that was spent to be holy, and love, and repent.

Help us Lord, to see what You did was to set us free to live with You for eternity. Help us receive as this is so much that You took on that cross and poured out blood. Help us fully get what happened that day, when You rose from that grave. When You rose and now, we have life to stay. Happy resurrection day Jesus, King of Kings, You surpassed our wildest dreams.

A FRIEND IN JESUS. Jesus is the best friend anyone could ask for. He is one who will forever keep His promises, won't ever give up, and He is always with you. No one compares to the one above. You may be at your lowest point and think no one is there for you, but I can assure you one thing, there is someone.

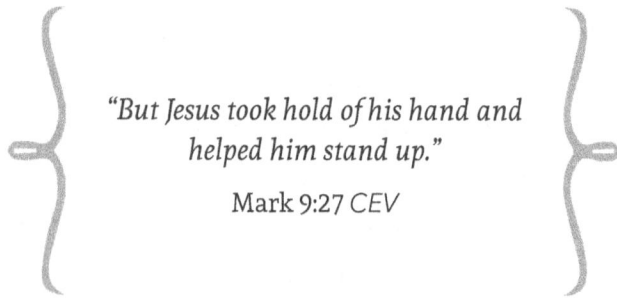

"But Jesus took hold of his hand and helped him stand up."

Mark 9:27 *CEV*

Don't give up.

The day is almost here. Don't give up. It's worth it you see. Don't give up. I know you have taken a beating. Don't give up. We are almost there. Don't give up. Heaven won't disappoint. Don't give up to live this life only to die and never be truly satisfied.

STRONG

STRESS. STRAIN. PRESSURE.

TENSION. Life's trials. Ups and downs.

My kids. My job. It all hit quick. I never chose to repent. I sat and loathed in hate and pity. What for? Why do we love to stay in our pity and hurt? Why must we, I ask Lord? This stress has torn my body down. It hit my soul and took me out. My spirit was getting weak in defeat. Then I woke up and saw.

He did not make us to live stressed, depressed, with high anxiety. He made us to live in communion with Thee.

Peace, love, and security.

Seasons may change, but His love remains the same. Battles seem long, but His fight and will are so strong. Go deep, weep, and don't keep those burdens or hate. Go forgive, and let go today, our Fathers love says it all. He paid the ultimate price, oh how it was bought. To live and not truly know, this life is not really our own. We owe it to Him, the one that endured it all.

Soak it in, this love that bears all.

> *"be fully capable of comprehending with all the saints (God's people) the width, and length, and height, and depth of His love [fully experiencing that amazing, endless love];"*
>
> Ephesians 3:18 *AMP*

Is anyone hurting, or lost, or simply just doesn't understand? Relationships can be hard. They can be really, really good, but they can be very, very hard.

My heart this morning, I wanted to share, anyone dealing with a loss in a relationship, I hope this helps.

Remember we always have our loving Father, the ultimate relationship. I pray a super natural blessing over all that are out there hurting.

Jesus can heal if you forgive, let go, and choose to go to the one that holds.

I pray for anyone going through a season of loss, grief, overwhelming sadness.

I pray Jesus comforts you.

All the trials. All the tragedy we may face. Lord, we only need to look to Your face. Your loving grace shines down and pours through the depths of our soul. When we stop and look, we know You hold all these trials we walk through. Help us to see them through with You by our side. With You as our guide. Your loving gracious will, only You provide. Help us see the way, help us see the light. It's only in our Father's eyes. Thank you, Jesus, for pulling us through. We will choose to honor and glorify You in these dark and sad days. It's our hope, it's Your power that reigns.

Hug your family, hug your friends. Choose to forgive the offense. You never know when the last day will be. Forgive, let go, and be free.

Control. Control. Control. Oh, how I love control. I love being in control. I love organizing, planning, and all of the above. Just being in control. I love it... until I don't. Control causes fear, worry, anxiety, perfection, and draining, overwhelming feelings of despair. Why do we feel we have to take it all on? Why do we feel like controlling it all until we fall apart?

If anyone struggles like I do, I pray a deep revelation, a deep peace, a deep surrender of letting go and letting the God of heaven control these things in your heart and in your life. Let go today and see His great grace.

"When my anxious thoughts multiply within me, Your comforts delight me."

Psalms 94:19 *AMP*

What do you honor? Maybe it's people. Maybe it's things, but today can we choose to honor our one true King.

Honor Him.

Respect Him in all that you do, and watch. Oh, watch how He turns your life to truth, to goodness, all of these things. Watch how He brings the hurt and the pain to the surface. Honor Him with all that you do and He will show you how honor looks on you.

I felt the Lord say, love Me more than anything. I said, I do. He said love Me more than you love yourself. That hit deep in my soul, my spirit. How many times do I think, how do I look, what am I going to do, I want this, I want that, me, me, me, me. I think we are naturally selfish in the flesh. I felt like I gave up everything and everyone, but I didn't give up me.

Thank you, Jesus, for this deep revelation. I love You more than myself. Die flesh, die. Spirit live.

Do you ever feel attacked, persecuted or misunderstood? I do. I have learned to let go of many hurts but some really cut deep. I believe I am my own worst enemy. Many things that people say compares to nothing I lay on myself.

I would say today, forgive yourself, love yourself and thank God for this creation He has made. It is perfect in His eyes.

When we cry out and don't get our way. When we try again the next day. When we go and replay all those times over and over and over again.

Wake us up.

Help us to let go and live again.

Let us see Your way, not ours. Help us to not hold a chip or stay in the dark. Call us out into the light and live. Help us see it's Yours to give.

It took me a lot of years after truly knowing that Jesus was to be number one in my life, to live and choose it daily. I still struggle some days to keep Him above my husband and children.

I pray for anyone today that has a hard time letting go of that tight grip we hold on our loved ones or even things, like sports or work, anything that stands in the way of Jesus being first in your life. I pray a deep, deep, surrender and peace, to let Jesus be the one that fills you up and allows everyone and everything else to flow from the relationship you have with Him.

Anyone struggling with the word family? What it means? What it doesn't mean? What it looks like or what it doesn't look like?

I would say family is not just your blood relatives. It's the people the Lord has placed in your life to do life with, to be there for you, to tell you truth, to never want to see you lose.

Don't get caught up with the word family. It could be that friend that never left, that child that you didn't birth, but now is your whole world.

God sees, He hears, He knows.

If your family is toxic, deadly, poisonous, harmful, destructive, or dangerous, you don't have to keep in that relationship only to get beaten down one more time.

Forgive them. Let them go. Walk away. Live in a whole new way.

Discernment may be one of the most valuable spiritual gifts to me. Discernment to be wise in judgment. Do you ever have a radar going off when you are about to do something you aren't supposed to do? Maybe you are traveling down the road and something tells you to stop or go the long way around. Maybe it's a person that you come in contact with and bam, it's like back up 10 feet. You just know to leave and walk away. Well, the good Lord gives us this gift to protect, guide, lead, and to keep us safe, if we yield and listen.

> *"My child, don't lose sight of common sense and discernment. Hang on to them, for they will refresh your soul. They are like jewels on a necklace. They keep you safe on your way, and your feet will not stumble. You can go to bed without fear; you will lie down and sleep soundly. You need not be afraid of sudden disaster or the destruction that comes upon the wicked, for the Lord is your security. He will keep your foot from being caught in a trap."*
>
> Proverbs 3:21-26 *NLT*

Faith over Fear.

I have heard it said many times, but tonight it stuck. Yeah, I run in fear. I let go and get out of control. I go into this mindless fearing pit like a flight risk. When did this hit? Where did this turn and go so bad from a thought into a worry, from a worry into a fear?

I believe it's the enemy's greatest weapon against us. If he keeps us bound in fear it's very difficult to fulfill our purpose. Oh, but faith comes like a light in the night, a trust, a belief, a hope, so firm and secure in everything, and the fear is gone and the faith is present, and I thank God when the faith is present and real in my life.

Though I may walk through the valley, Lord, You are always with me.

That's enough. You are always and forever with me. I'm praying for anyone struggling with fear. It's so real. Don't run, don't hide. Stand up to it today. Ask God for help to turn and walk away from that fear and slay, slay, slay. That's the will of God.

Peace, He leaves with us, take it, have it, it's yours.

With all the opposition, all the hate, all the opinions and race, it seems this world is quick to tear down what Jesus came to save. I can't help but wonder with this stye in my eye, is there something I am judging too hard, staying offended, not letting go of and forgiving well? Is there something in there that I can't tell? It's easy for me to see others failures and faults, but when it comes to me it's like it's no thought.

Help me Father, keep me pure. Help me repent and see more. Help me Father, for I have sinned. Help me see like You see, and forgive.

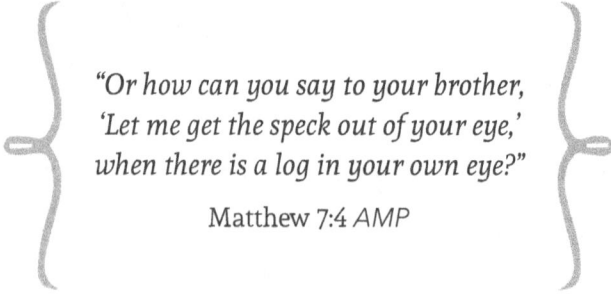

"Or how can you say to your brother, 'Let me get the speck out of your eye,' when there is a log in your own eye?"

Matthew 7:4 *AMP*

Are you feeling distracted, lost, lonely, or scared? Distraction brings forth all these feelings of unwell. Distraction is said to be a misdirection, disorder, or confusion. I feel all of them and start fuming. It agitates and rears up on those deadlines. It agitates when I believe everything is fine. Distraction is easy to fall into but a beast when trying to be focused on mighty things that are proven. I pray for anyone distracted today. I pray you see with eyes of grace and faith. I pray that distraction leaves and you can be focused on those mighty, heavenly things.

Life is like a breath, a pass of time, a wink, a close of an eye. Life is so precious. So, why do we run? Why do we fight? Why do we go all day and never see the sight, the prize, the one at hand? How can we walk 10 miles and never know Your plans?

Help us sit, help us stay, help us see Your loving face. Help us Father to see this life is not eternity. We will be there one day, yes, but help us live our best before You take us home. Show us Your grace and throne.

ABOUT THE AUTHORS:

ADDIE WHITTAKER is a 14-year-old from Bourbon, Missouri. She enjoys riding her horses, Freedom and True. She also enjoys playing softball with some of her favorite people. Addie loves to share about Jesus and always wants to go further in his love.

LACEY WHITTAKER is the Founder of True Love Ministries. She yearns to flow only from the heart of Jesus. She lives in Bourbon, MO with her husband Justin and two daughters Addie and Liv. Her heart is for everyone to know that the most important relationship you can have is the one on one with our Father.

www.ingramcontent.com/pod-product-compliance
Lightning Source LLC
Chambersburg PA
CBHW070725130626
46553CB00005B/2149